Extreme Skateboarding

by Pat Ryan

Content Consultant:
Jim Fitzpatrick
International Association of Skateboard Companies

CAPSTONE PRESS

MANKATO, MINNESOTA

CAPSTONE PRESS

818 North Willow Street • Mankato, Minnesota 56001
http://www.capstone-press.com

Printed in the United States of America.

Library of Congress Cataloging-in-Publication Data
Ryan, Pat
    Extreme skateboarding/by Pat Ryan.
    p. cm. -- (Extreme sports)
    Includes bibliographical references and index.
    Summary: Describes the history, equipment, and contemporary practice of extreme skateboarding.
    ISBN 1-56065-535-6
    1. Skateboarding--Juvenile literature. [1. Skateboarding.] I. Title.
II. Series.

GV859.8.R93 1998
796.22--dc21

                        97-9396
                          CIP
                          AC

Editorial credits
Editor, Cara Van Voorst; Cover design, Timothy Halldin; Photo research, Michelle L. Norstad
Photo credits
Patrick Batchelder, 32
Grant Brittain, cover, 6, 9, 10, 12, 16, 22, 24, 26, 29, 30, 36, 44
Jeff Divine, 38
FPG/Jim Cummins, 47; Michael Kornafel, 43; John Terence Turner, 14, 18
Rutger Geerling, 20
MSI/Richard Cheski, 4
Visuals Unlimited/WM Ormerod, 34

Table of Contents

Chapter 1

Skateboarding

Skateboarders, or skaters, ride skateboards on or over obstacles. An obstacle is an object that blocks or changes a path. Obstacles include ramps, rails, curbs, or jumps. Skaters use one foot to push the board forward. Then they place both feet on the board. Skaters use their body weight to turn the board and to balance.

Skateboarding takes place on city streets or at skate parks. A skate park is a place built just for skateboarding. It includes obstacles that are modeled after swimming pools, culverts, and other street shapes. A culvert is a large, concrete pipe. A skate park also has ramps. A ramp is a sloping surface linking one level with another. Skate parks can be indoors, outdoors, or both.

Skateboarders also compete in contests as amateurs or professionals. Amateur skaters compete only for pleasure. Professional skaters are highly skilled. They receive money for competing in contests.

Skateboarders compete in contests as amateurs or professionals.

Most extreme skateboarding takes place at skate parks.

Extreme Skateboarding

Extreme skateboarding is more difficult than regular skateboarding. Most extreme skateboarding takes place at skate parks.

Extreme skateboarders perform many different tricks. They try to perform more difficult tricks than other skateboarders. They also try to perform a series of tricks. This series is called a run.

Some common streetstyle tricks are ollies and grinds. Streetstyle is a skateboard style performed on obstacles that are common on city streets. These include curbs and handrails. An ollie is a jump into the air without using hands to hold onto the board. A grind is a trick performed by skating across an object on the board's axles.

Many vertical style tricks include aerials. Vertical style is a skateboad style performed on vertical ramps. An aerial is a trick a skater performs while in the air. Some extreme skateboarders spin one and one-half times in midair.

Skateboarding Styles

Freestyle, streetstyle, miniature ramp, and vertical ramp are four styles of skateboarding. Freestyle skateboarding is the oldest and most graceful of the skateboarding styles. Extreme freestyle skaters usually skateboard on a flat area, like a parking lot. Sometimes they skateboard on outdoor basketball courts. Freestyle skaters use many gymnastics moves. For example, a freestyler may do a handstand on the board.

Streetstyle skateboarding is popular because it can be done almost anywhere. Extreme streetstyle skaters use streets, alleys, and other parts of cities. Extreme streetstyle skaters have mastered the basic moves. They look for more difficult rides. They skateboard on handrails, stairs, fences, curbs, and concrete banks. Most skate parks have streetstyle obstacles for boarders to practice on.

Miniature-ramp style takes place on a plywood course with many levels and mini-ramps. Plywood is layers of wood glued together. The mini-ramps are different heights. Some ramps are harder than others for tricks. Mini-ramps are usually found at skate parks.

Vertical style skateboarding began in empty outdoor swimming pools. Vertical style is named for the vertical ramp. Vertical means straight up. There are two types of vertical ramps. One vertical ramp is based on the shape of a

A grind is a streetstyle trick.

A half-pipe ramp is U-shaped. Extreme skaters perform tricks in the air at the top of the walls.

swimming pool. True verticals have walls 11 feet (3.4 meters) high. Skaters call them vert ramps.

The second vert ramp is called a half-pipe. A half-pipe ramp is U-shaped. Skateboarders skate down one wall and up the other. Extreme skaters perform tricks in the air at the top of the walls.

The Extreme Skateboarders

Most extreme skateboarders are professionals. Extreme boarders try many new tricks. They try to create difficult tricks, too.

Extreme skateboarders exercise to stay in shape. They practice often. This helps them improve their skills and perform the best tricks.

Many extreme skateboarders practice all four skateboarding styles. But they usually have one or two favorite styles. Most extreme skaters concentrate on streetstyle and vert style. These are the styles judged at competitions. A competition is a contest between two or more skaters.

Extreme skateboarders like Colin McKay are professionals.

Chapter 2
History of Skateboarding

In the 1950s and early 1960s surfing became a popular sport. It was a fad with young people across North America. A fad is something that is very popular for a short time. Young skateboarders found they could copy some surfboarding moves. It was like surfing on land. Soon thousands of people were skateboarding.

The Skateboard

People first began skateboarding in the 1950s. The first skateboard was probably a scooter with the pushbar broken off. A scooter is a board with two wheels and a pushbar. The rider stands on the board with one foot and pushes with the other.

Young skateboarders found they could copy some surfboarding moves.

Companies began making thousands of skateboards. The early boards were narrow slabs of wood with metal roller-skate wheels. The early boards were dangerous. A crack in the sidewalk could stop the wheels from turning. Even a pebble could stop the wheels. This caused accidents. Safety experts wanted to stop the fad.

By the middle of the 1960s, clay wheels replaced the original steel wheels. Skaters could balance easier on skateboards with clay wheels. Skateboarding became very popular again.

In 1972, skateboarder Frank Nasworthy invented the urethane wheel. Urethane is a type of hard rubber or plastic. Urethane wheels are softer than metal wheels. The invention of urethane wheels started the second 10 years of skateboarding history. The newer, softer wheels made the ride smoother and safer. The board easily rolled over small rocks and cracks in the cement.

Some safety experts wanted to stop the skateboarding fad. They thought it was too dangerous.

Skate Parks

A new generation of skaters became interested in skateboarding in the 1970s. More than 300 skate parks were built all over North America.

The skate parks offered skaters a safer place to skateboard. Ramps and other obstacles were built and maintained for the skaters.

Today, skate parks are still popular with skateboarders. Skaters meet other skaters at skate parks. They learn new tricks from each other.

Early Competitions

Eventually, skateboarders began to set up local competitions at the skate parks. Athletes from a town or city competed against each other. An athlete is a person trained in a sport or a game.

Skateboard manufacturers realized that sponsoring competitions or skateboarders was a good way to advertise. Soon the competitions became larger. More people began watching and competing.

Skaters meet other skaters at skate parks. They learn new tricks from each other.

Chapter 3

Extreme Competition

Skateboarding is more popular today than it has ever been. The number of active skateboarders in North America is about six and one-half million. Worldwide, another two million people are skateboarders. Many of these skaters compete against one another. The 1996 Summer Olympics in Atlanta, Georgia, featured a skateboard demonstration.

Extreme skateboarders like to try new, difficult tricks. To do so, they build more difficult obstacles. Most championship competitions use a ramp 48 feet (14.4 meters) wide and 11 feet (3.3 meters) tall. Each skater has 45 seconds to do as many tricks as possible. In a high-air contest, skaters try to jump as high as they can. Some skaters have reached 10 feet (three meters) above the ramp. Air means the height and length of time a skater is off the ground.

Extreme skateboarders like Andy MacDonald like to try new and difficult tricks.

Skaters like Tony Hawk have reached 10 feet above the ramp.

Rules and Judging Standards

Skateboarding competitions are all different. Most competitions include streetstyle. Many also include freestyle and vert style. Some basic things are the same. For example, most competitions require skaters to wear protective safety gear. Skaters are usually given 45 to 90 seconds to complete a run.

Judges use a 10-point system for each run. A rating of 10 is the highest possible score. Judges make decisions based on four main standards. They judge how difficult the trick is and how well the skater controls the board. They also judge the smoothness of the run and the number of tricks performed.

The Monster World Cup

Many professional skateboarders attend the Monster World Cup in Germany. Skateboarders from all over the world come to compete. The competition is held once a year and lasts for a weekend. Hundreds of skaters compete. Only a few of the skateboarders make it to the final rounds. The winners of the Monster World Cup receive prizes and money.

The X Games

The Extreme Games is a competition. It includes exciting sports like in-line skating, BMX bike racing, and bungee jumping.

The Extreme Games is also called the X Games. There are Summer and Winter X Games. Skateboarding is part of the Summer X Games. The athletes try to win prize money.

The X Games includes two major skateboarding categories. They are vert and street. One of the most popular street events features a 40-foot-long (12-meter) rail. Skateboarders jump with their skateboard onto the rail. Then they slide down it.

There is also a pyramid ramp. It has quarter-pipe ramps on four sides and a platform in the middle. Skaters skate up one side and drop onto another. Skaters have performed high-scoring tricks on this ramp.

One of the most popular X Games street events features a 40-foot-long (12-meter) rail.

Skaters can choose between many different ramps and streetstyle obstacles at the X Games.

Chapter 4
Equipment

Extreme skateboarders need a good skateboard, shoes, and safety equipment to practice their sport. They use the same basic equipment that regular boarders use. Some professional skaters help design new skateboards.

Parts of a Skateboard

The deck, wheels, and trucks are the three main parts of a skateboard. Many skateboarders buy each part separately. They try to make the skateboard fit their style of boarding.

The board that skaters stand on is called the deck. There are different deck types for different types of skateboarding. Most decks are made of maple plywood.

The deck, wheels, and trucks are the three main parts of a skateboard.

The truck is the part of a skateboard that attaches the wheels to the deck.

Today's skateboarders use urethane wheels. The wheels come in different sizes. Skaters can turn more easily with small, soft wheels. Hard wheels are best for speed and control. Many vert skateboarders prefer the harder wheels. They need speed to perform their ramp tricks.

A truck is the part of a skateboard that attaches the wheels to the board. Skaters use trucks to help steer the board. The trucks turn on a kingpin. A kingpin is a post in the center of a truck.

Old-School and New-School Boards

There are old-school and new-school skateboards. These names refer to both skateboards and styles of skateboarding.

Old-school skaters may use boards with wide decks. The old-school deck has a wide tail and a small nose. The tail is the back of the board. The nose is the front. An old-school board lasts a long time.

The new-school rider has a new style of board. It is built for indoor skate parks. The new board is low to the ground for better balance. A new-school board gains speed quickly. The board has a thin deck.

Gear

Other skateboarding gear is also important. Some old-school skaters prefer hightop shoes. They think hightops help keep their ankles straight. Most skaters today wear low top shoes.

Most skateboarders also use grip tape. Grip tape is like sandpaper. It helps keep a boarder's feet from slipping off the board. Many boards come with grip tape already attached.

Chapter 5
Safety

All skateboarders need three things for safe boarding. First, they need protective clothing. Second, they must know how to fall. Finally, skateboarders must know how to take care of a skateboard.

There are several kinds of protective clothing and safety equipment for skateboarders. Most big competitions require skaters to wear safety gear. They wear helmets, elbow pads, knee pads, and wrist guards. This equipment helps prevent scrapes and broken bones. Some skaters also wear gloves. Gloves protect the hands from cuts and scrapes.

Skateboarders must know how to fall as safely as possible. Beginning boarders sometimes try to stop a fall with their hands. This leads to broken wrists and hands. Long-time skaters hold their elbows close to their chests and roll onto their shoulders. They may get some scrapes, but they rarely break bones.

Most extreme skateboarders wear helmets, elbow pads, and knee pads.

Vert style skateboarders should always wear knee pads. The best way to fall on a vert ramp is to slide on the front of the knees.

A skatcboard is an extreme skateboarder's tool. Taking good care of that tool is important for good rides and for safety. Extreme skaters make sure all of the screws on the skateboard are tight. Wheels need replacing from time to time. A board that breaks or does not work properly is dangerous.

Where to Skateboard

Many extreme skateboarders practice at skate parks. Some also practice on city streets. It is important to obey city skateboarding laws. A few careless people could cause a city to ban skateboarding on all of its streets.

Extreme skateboarders also try to practice with other people. If someone gets hurt, the other skaters can call for help.

Extreme skateboarders try to practice with other people.

Truck

Deck

Helmet

Elbow Pad

Equipment

Urethane wheels

Knee Pad

Glove

Practice Makes Perfect

Extreme skateboarders practice many hours a day. They never try tricks without practicing all the skills needed to do them. A new trick takes hours of practice to perfect.

Each new trick is practiced one step at a time. After each step, a boarder tries all of the new steps together.

Daring tricks and big competitions are the fun parts of extreme skateboarding. But experienced boarders put safety first.

Extreme skateboarders practice many hours a day.

Words to Know

aerial (AIR-ee-uhl)—a trick performed in midair

athlete (ATH-leet)—a person trained in a sport or game

competition (kom-puh-TISH-uhn)—a contest between two or more athletes

deck (DEK)—the board part of a skateboard, often made from maple plywood

Extreme Games (ek-STREEM GAMES)—an extreme skateboarding competition featuring many sports; also known as the X Games

freestyle (FREE-stile)—a skateboarding style that includes many gymnastics moves

grind (GRINDE)—a trick performed by skating across an object on a skateboard's axles

grip tape (GRIP TAYP)—tape attached to skateboards that helps keep skaters' feet from slipping

half-pipe ramp (HAF-pipe RAMP)—a U-shaped ramp with high walls

miniature ramp (MIN-ee-uh-chur RAMP)—a small ramp often built with many different levels

miniature ramp style (MIN-ee-uh-chur RAMP STILE)—a skateboading style performed on miniature ramps

ollie (AH-lee)—a jump into the air without using hands to hold onto the board

run (RUHN)—a series of skateboard tricks

skate park (SKAYT PARK)—a place built for skateboarding; it includes ramps and streetstyle obstacles

streetstyle (STREET-stile)—a skateboard style performed on obstacles that are common on city streets such as curbs and handrails

truck (TRUHK)—the part of a skateboard that attaches the wheels to the deck

urethane wheel (YOOR-uh-thayn WEEL)—a skateboard wheel made from hard rubber

vertical ramp (VUR-tuh-kuhl RAMP)—a ramp with walls 11 feet (3.3 meters) high; based on the shape of a swimming pool

vertical style (VUR-tuh-kuhl STILE)—a skateboard style performed on vertical ramps

To Learn More

Reiser, Howard. *Skateboarding*. New York: Franklin Watts, 1989.

Hills, Galvin. *Skateboarding*. All Action Series. Minneapolis: Lerner Publications, 1993.

Jay, Jackson. *Skateboarding Basics*. Mankato, Minn.: Capstone Press, 1996.

Shoemaker, Joel. *Skateboarding Streetstyle*. Action Sports. Mankato, Minn.: Capstone Press, 1995.

You can read articles about skateboarding in *Transworld Skateboarding* and *Thrasher* magazines.

Useful
Addresses

International Association of Skateboard Companies
P.O. Box 37
Santa Barbara, CA 93116

California Amateur Skateboard League
P.O. Box 30004
San Bernardino, CA 92413

Thrasher **Magazine**
c/o High Speed Publications
P.O. Box 24592
San Francisco, CA 94124

Transworld Skateboarding **Magazine**
353 Airport Road
Oceanside, CA 92054

Internet Sites

ESPNET SportsZone:Skateboarding
http://espn.sportszone.com/editors/xgames/skate/
    index.html

Skate FAQ
http://web.cps.msu.edu/~dunharnda/dw/faq.html

SKATEBOARD.COM
http://www.skateboard.com/tydu/skatebrd/
    skate.html

IASC
http://www.tumyeto.com/tydu/skatebrd/
    organizations/iasc.html

Extreme
http://www.extreme-sports.com/index.html

ExtremeSports
http://www.burstgum.com/extreme/index.html

Index